THE LIBRARY OF WHY?™

Why Can Airplanes Fly?

Marian B. Jacobs, Ph.D.

The Rosen Publishing Group's
PowerKids Press™
New York

For my grandsons, Carlos and Gianni.

Published in 1999 by The Rosen Publishing Group, Inc.
29 East 21st Street, New York, NY 10010

First Edition

Book Design: Danielle Primiceri

Photo Credits and Photo Illustrations: Cover © Arthur Tilley/FPG International; p. 4 © Corbis-Bettmann; p. 7 © Scott Barrow/International Stock; pp. 8, 15 © Ryan Giuliani; p. 11 © Frank Cezus/FPG International and 1996 PhotoDisc; p. 12 © Michael Lichter/International Stock; pp. 16, 20 © Maratea/International Stock; p. 19 © 1996 PhotoDisc; p. 22 © Michael Agliolo/International Stock.

Jacobs, Marian B.
    Why can airplanes fly? / by Marian B. Jacobs.
        p.   cm.— (The library of why?)
    Includes index.
    Summary: Provides answers to such flight-related questions as "How do airplane wings work?" and "What is thrust?"
    ISBN 0-8239-5274-6
    1. Flight—Juvenile literature. 2. Air flow—Juvenile literature. [1. Flight—Miscellanea. 2. Questions and answers.] I. Title. II. Series: Jacobs, Marian B. Library of why?
TL547.J33 1998
629.132—dc21   98-9258
                                                                                          CIP
                                                                                          AC

Manufactured in the United States of America

Contents

What Is Aviation?

People have always wanted to fly. Some people tried to copy birds by building huge wings. But the wings didn't help them fly. Early flyers didn't understand the science of flying, called **aviation** (AY-vee-AY-shun).

In the early 1900s two brothers, Orville and Wilbur Wright, did **experiments** (ek-SPEH-rih-ments) to figure out the secret of aviation. What they discovered allowed them to fly. On December 17, 1903, they made the first **powered** (POW-erd) flight. It lasted twelve seconds, and the plane flew 121 feet.

◀ *This is the Wright brothers' famous plane, the Wright Flyer 1.*

5

What Is Flight?

Insects, birds, and bats are the only creatures that can truly fly. This means that they have enough power to lift themselves off the ground and move through the air under their own control. People don't have that power. We have to fly in airplanes. But airplanes are big and heavy, so why can they fly?

Flight is made possible when the wings of a bird, insect, or airplane push against air. The air pushes back. This action and **reaction** (ree-AK-shun) has enough **force** (FORSS) to allow the bird, insect, or airplane to fly.

An airplane is supported by air the way a boat is supported by water. ▶

What Is Air Pressure?

Air **pressure** (PREH-sher) is the force that air puts on the things around it. Air pressure pushes up on the bottom of an airplane wing and allows it to fly. This experiment will show you what air pressure is:

○ Stuff a tissue in the bottom of a clear glass.

○ Turn the glass upside down over a bowl of water. Push down on the glass. You will feel **resistance** (re-ZIS-tants). This is because air in the glass is pushing against the water in the bowl. That is air pressure.

○ Lift the glass out of the water. The tissue is dry because air stopped the water from touching it.

How Do Birds Fly?

We have learned a lot about flight by watching birds. Birds are built for flying. They have strong chest muscles to flap their wings. Their bones are **hollow** (HAH-loh) so they weigh very little.

A bird flaps its wings to make air move faster over the top of its wings. This makes the air pressure on top of its wings less than below the wings. More air pressure below the wings pushes up on the wings and makes it possible for the bird to fly. The tail feathers help the bird **steer** (STEER), just like the tail of an airplane helps it steer.

Birds don't just flap their wings up and down. Their wings flap in a circular motion, which allows them to fly. ▶

FLOW OF AIR

LIFT

FLOW OF AIR

What Is Lift?

The difference in air pressure that we've learned about creates an upward force called lift. Airplane wings don't flap to create lift. They have a special shape that makes lift happen. The top of a plane's wing is curved and the bottom is flatter. The curved top lets air pass over it faster than under it. This makes the air pressure below the wing greater than the pressure above the wing. This creates lift. And even though the airplane is big and heavy, the lift created is enough to make the plane fly.

◄ *The weight of the plane is like a force pushing down. Lift works directly against this force and allows the plane to fly.*

How Can You Create Lift at Home?

This experiment shows how moving air allows a plane to fly.

○ Cut a strip of paper about 6 inches long by 2 inches wide.

○ Hold the shorter edge below your bottom lip. Let the paper hang over your fingers and chin.

○ Blow gently across the top of the paper, and it will lift.

The slower moving air underneath the paper lifts it up just like the slower moving air under an airplane wing lifts up the airplane.

How Do Airplanes Move Through the Air?

Thrust (THRUST) is a force that moves something, or changes its direction. Thrust is the force that allows the pilot to change the speed of the plane. A plane's thrust usually comes from two different sources: **propellers** (pruh-PEL-erz) or jet engines.

Propellers spin around and pull planes through the air. Jet engines push out hot gases, which causes the plane to move forward very fast. Thrust works against a force called drag. Drag is the force of air pushing against the plane as it moves forward.

◀ *Planes used by the U.S. Armed Forces, such as the Stealth B-2 Bomber, have special engines that provide more thrust than regular planes.*

What Are the Parts of an Airplane?

Airplanes are built to fly. The wings create lift and allow the plane to leave the ground. Jet engines or propellers give thrust. All of these parts are attached to the body of the plane, called the **fuselage** (FYOO-seh-laj). A fuselage carries the crew, passengers, and cargo.

There are controls to steer the plane, and a **rudder** (RUH-der) on the tail for turning. Flaps on the wings help control takeoff and landing. And there is landing gear with strong wheels that the airplane uses to take off and land. All of these parts work together and allow the plane to fly under the control of the pilot.

Planes are specially built so that all the parts work well together. This way the plane can fly smoothly. ▶

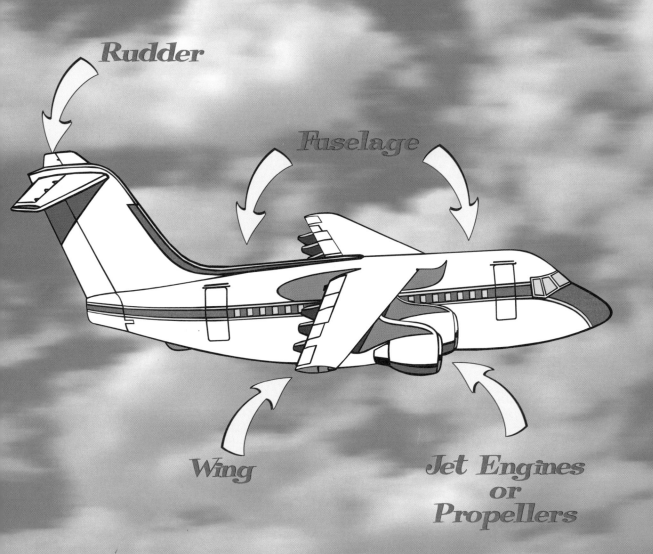

Rudder

Fuselage

Wing

Jet Engines
or
Propellers

How Are Some Airplanes Different?

You may see many different kinds of planes in the sky or on TV. But no matter what a plane looks like, it still has all the things it needs to fly.

Planes that do different jobs need special shapes or **equipment** (ee-KWIP-ment) in order to do those jobs. Some planes can land on water. They have special landing gear called **pontoons** (pon-TOONZ). Some planes are specially built to fly right into thunderstorms so they can study the weather. Other planes can skim across a lake or ocean and pick up large amounts of water. These planes then drop the water on forest fires.

◀ *Special planes and trained people do stunts at airshows around the world.*

How Have Airplanes Changed Our World?

Since 1903, airplanes have been made bigger, better, and faster. Large jets can carry more than 400 people at a time to places all around the world. Before airplanes, it would take days, weeks, even months for people to travel to different states or countries. But today, we can fly around the world in a matter of hours. Food and medicine can be sent to people who need help. Airplanes have made our world a better place.

Web Sites:

You can learn more about aviation at these Web sites:
http://hawaii.cogsci.uiuc.edu/invent/air_main.shtml
http://worldflight.org/youcansoar/resources/fly.how.html

Glossary

aviation (AY-vee-AY-shun) The science of flying.

equipment (ee-KWIP-ment) The items needed to do a certain job.

experiment (ek-SPEH-rih-ment) To do tests as you try to figure something out.

force (FORSS) Something in nature that causes motion or change.

fuselage (FYOO-seh-laj) The body of a plane that carries passengers, crew, and cargo.

hollow (HAH-loh) To be empty in the middle.

pontoon (pon-TOON) A flat-bottomed float attached to a seaplane that allows the plane to take off and land on water.

powered (POW-erd) Something that moves with the help of an engine.

pressure (PREH-sher) A force put on something.

propeller (pruh-PEL-er) A spinning blade that pulls an airplane through the air.

reaction (ree-AK-shun) An action in response to a force.

resistance (re-ZIS-tants) A stopping force put on one thing by another.

rudder (RUH-der) A flat piece of wood or metal that helps steer a plane.

steer (STEER) To direct or guide movement.

thrust (THRUST) A force against something that moves it.

Index